Motivational Murder:
The Seven Worst Mistakes Leaders Make

Bobby Hoffman, Ph.D.

A•P Attribution Press

Attribution Press
P.O. Box 623342
Oviedo, FL 32762
www.attributionpress.com

Ordering Information:
Quantity sales. Special discounts are available on quantity purchases by corporations, associations, and others. For details, contact the publisher at the address above.
Orders by U.S. trade bookstores and wholesalers. Please contact hackyourmotivation@gmail.com

Printed in the United States of America
Cover Design: Hannah Carter

Publisher's Cataloging-in-Publication data
Hoffman, Bobby.
Motivational Murder: The seven worst mistakes leaders make/Bobby Hoffman
ISBN 978-0-9988457-0-8
1.—Motivation—Leadership. 2. Psychology 3. Self-help

To all the crappy bosses who needlessly squash the passion and ruin the motivation of dedicated employees

Motivational Murder

An important message to readers

Thank you for ordering *Motivational Murder*. Like the book *Hack Your Motivation*, the information here is designed to enhance your personal and professional success. Instead of focusing on Hacks (strategies and skills needed to efficiently reach your goals), here you will learn how to diagnose, assess, and avoid toxic company and work cultures. The knowledge described in both books is exclusively based on human motivation research from the fields of psychology, education, business, athletics, and neuroscience.

When you master the content in this book you will be able to:

- Determine your fit within the culture of a current or future employer
- Ask insightful interview questions to detect leadership styles
- Implement strategies to overcome micro-managers and bad bosses
- Identify the reasons for employee apathy and disengagement
- Demonstrate workplace behaviors conducive to promotion and personal growth
- Coach and motivate constituents and coworkers
- Go to work feeling revitalized and refreshed

If you think this book (or any other) reveals magic formulas to instantly transform your work life from frustration to elation: *think again*. There are no instant solutions despite what authors of other motivation books may promise. The difference here is complete reliance upon scientifically-supported solutions rather than mere opinion. When you follow the recommendations within, you will achieve success with less effort, more vigor, and better results. Ultimately, you will be able to discriminate between effective leadership and slick impersonators and learn how to avoid the seven worst mistakes *uninformed* leaders make.

April 4, 2017

Dr. Bobby Hoffman
hackyourmotivation@gmail.com

Self-motivation is essential for personal success, however as parents, partners, friends, coworkers, and motivational thought leaders, we are often equally concerned or held accountable for the well-being of others. As such, we may volunteer our time or be drafted to help those around us. Depending on your inclinations and chosen profession, your reputation or livelihood may be staked upon those you lead. This is often the case for many professionals including teachers, psychologists, coaches, and most corporate executives. Even if you aren't obliged to help others excel, your leadership competency will be enhanced if you avoid the most common motivational pitfalls that minimally disrupt performance and in the worst case, derail otherwise successful careers. Are you prepared to dedicate your motivational effort to the service of others?

***

Leadership Mistake #1

Motivation can be mandated

I often bring a magic wand to my face-to-face seminars and university classes. The audience usually emits a loud chuckle when I ask for a volunteer and proceed to wave my magic wand over their head and declare them "*motivated.*" While this approach is conceivably absurd, some motivation books imply that by simply following the author's guidance you will instantly become motivated. Authors of these books declare their methods are proven formulas: when one explicitly follows their suggestions, intense drive and immediate success will result…leading to massive wealth.

Motivation in a box!

These dubious claims are usually substantiated by describing a record of personal achievement from a highly charismatic and knowledgeable individual who has succeeded in one field and believes their experience is sufficient to motivate people in diverse disciplines, careers, and life situations. Upon examining these claims in detail, we usually find little knowledge of *actual* motivational science or any replicable evidence to support the author's suggestions. Most of the "secrets" revolve around speaking, thinking, and acting like the author: "do as I do and you too will succeed" is essentially their mantra and motivational wisdom. Unfortunately, these authors fail to realize that motivation cannot be mandated, regardless whether using a magic wand or just words in a book or speech.

There are several problems with motivation bequeathed by others. First, the *"expert"* is operating under the premise that a strategy will work for you because it worked for them. Many motivational prognosticators are highly successful in their own careers, but rely almost exclusively on private, untestable approaches that may not necessarily apply to others in similar situations. Unless the approach has undergone rigorous scientific testing with controlled conditions, there is no accurate way to attest to the superiority or even the efficacy of their methods. If you see or hear any author or speaker suggest their methods are *"proven"* **- run the other way**.

Second, any reputable researcher defends the notion that nothing is ever considered absolute proof because contradictory evidence can falsify any theory. Neither the popularity of ideas nor the source of the rhetoric determines merit. If you recall from high school history, for centuries many people believed the earth was flat and slavery was an appropriate way to staff a growing colonial business. In the 1800's medical illnesses were inappropriately diagnosed by examining the shape of the patient's skull. These prevailing theories and strategies of the time were debunked when undiscovered evidence was subsequently realized. Ironically, when a motivational huckster's *"proven formula"* fails to work, the user is often blamed for not following the prescriptive formula or chastised because they are a "non-believer." Third, as readers of *Hack Your Motivation* will learn, diagnosing and mediating motivational challenges cannot be achieved through generalizations. Motivation is constantly in flux based on the task at hand, the performer's beliefs, and the venue conditions. Beyond that, motives rapidly evolve owing to task progress or failure. In other words, motivational solutions will change based on the person and the problem.

Unfortunately, many overzealous and uninformed leaders in classrooms, homes, and workplaces adopt methods designed to accomplish the same goals as the misinformed motivation experts who tout their claims in TED Talks, books, and late-night infomercials. Often relying on authority, these well-intentioned leaders consider themselves *"coaches."* They identify motivational deficiencies, provide support and encouragement, and describe idealistic behaviors implying absolutely anyone can magically transform performance. Their approach is not much different than my magic wand during presentations. Sadly, the same fallacy that disavows the shrewd motivational imposters applies here. Personal motivation cannot be authorized by others, unless the person who is trying to motivate you has the same unique experiences, beliefs, and opportunities as you---a logistical and scientific *impossibility*.

Beware of:
- **Proven formulas**
- **Instant results**
- **Avoid "simple" or "secret" solutions**

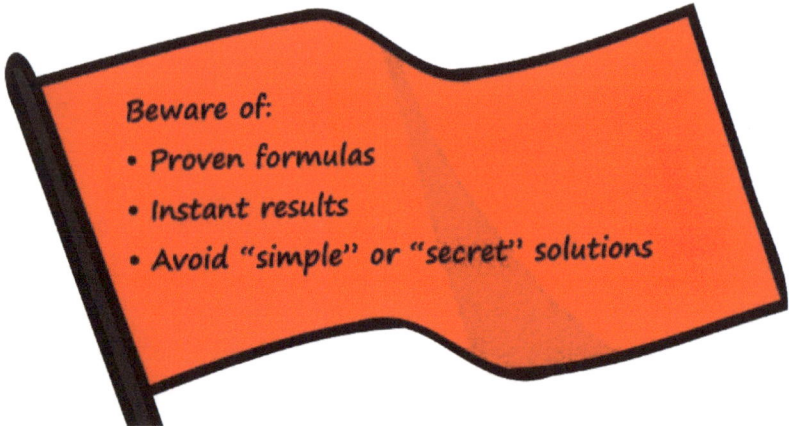

Despite the limitations of a universal approach to motivating others, individuals can enhance professional success by observing and modeling the behavior of skilled leaders. First, realize that behaviors evaluated as appropriate and desirable in one organizational setting may not apply universally. Thus, you should be sure you model organizationally appropriate behaviors. Second, regardless of company culture, individual success requires a willingness to accept constructive criticism. Perceive feedback not as a sign of weakness or a judgmental evaluation, rather as opportunity to learn and expedite personal growth. Solidifying your future in an organization takes work and effort.

Part of the challenge is not allowing yourself to fall into the trap of automatically exhibiting comfortable and habitual patterns of behavior. This means resisting the urge to become defensive when someone offers honest feedback. Finally, if you are the coach, be sure your message to constituents and colleagues is clear and specific, with care taken to avoid interpretation for hidden meanings. The individual must perceive your message as relevant and you, the leader, as a credible and trustworthy source or the probability of serious consideration or even temporary adoption of suggestions will be extremely limited.

***

Leadership Mistake #2

Inconsistency between motivational messages and action

I recently attended a 90-minute strategic planning presentation at a prominent university. The speaker was a college Dean, who is accountable to about 150 faculty and staff. I noticed two very clear messages in her speech. First, she outlined goals for the upcoming academic year and emphatically stressed the need to increase student enrollment. Second, it *appeared* faculty were empowered and would be held accountable for achieving the objectives set forth in the presentation. I was puzzled because while advocating the involvement of faculty to achieve the college mission, the speaker repeatedly used the words "*you will*" when referring to desired outcomes. I could not understand how faculty were expected to feel empowered while at the same time being mandated to achieve what appeared to be many non-negotiable goals.

Upon further investigation, I learned the organization had recently conducted a climate survey. The survey revealed only 44% of respondents agreed administrators resolved problems honestly, effectively, quickly, and collaboratively, while a paltry 27% believed supervisors made decisions without regard to politics and favoritism. A whopping 67% of respondents disagreed when asked whether they thought administrators were transparent and the information shared was complete. The picture became clearer. Despite the rhetoric about the importance of faculty contributions during the presentation, the survey findings seemed to indicate faculty felt marginalized (at least anonymously). I also discovered the university employed four times more staff and administrators than faculty members. A mismatch between what was advocated during the meeting and day-to-day leadership behavior was apparent.

After speaking to faculty, I learned what I feared most—a lack of alignment between what was said and what was done. Based upon confluent research across industries and professions, lack of leadership credibility is one of the most frequently cited reasons for employee disengagement. Consequences of disengagement include indifferent workers who call in sick more frequently, have questionable organizational commitment, complain frequently, and exhibit a general unwillingness to challenge the status quo. The ambiguity between strategy and behavior is toxic because it confuses employees who cannot decipher how effort should be invested when messages conflict. Often, the discrepancies between what leaders **say** and what leaders **do** breeds mistrust among those being led. The mistrust nurtures an *"us versus them"* mentality manifested in reluctance to collaborate and decreased motivation to excel. When people are uncertain about loyalties or confused about what behaviors are appropriate, complacency tends to follow.

- *No time to ask questions*
- *Many open positions*
- *High turnover*

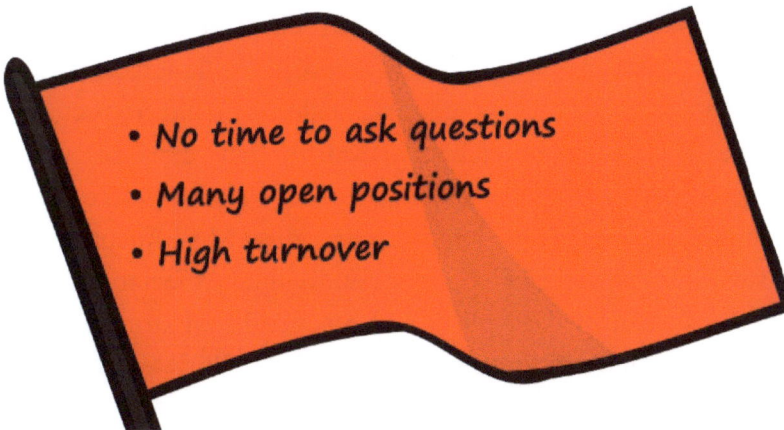

The key to creating a culture of trust begins by providing clear and unambiguous messages. In turn, leader actions should mirror communications to show organizational commitment, and to establish routine and predictable behaviors among followers. Leaders should realize actions represent the public face of the organization and their behavior is a benchmark for frontline employees to model. Thus, if an organization is espousing employee development as a key metric of success, employees should receive evaluative, relevant, and clear-cut feedback encouraging and rewarding personal development. More importantly, leaders should share news and policy changes with the entire organization, avoiding selective withholding of information that may foster a culture of perceived "haves" and "have nots." Removing unnecessary mystery concerning organizational operations promotes trust. If the person who is the target of a motivational message has any suspicion or perception of a leader's hidden agenda resistance will result and inhibit the climate leaders hope to cultivate.

Motivational Murder

The most reliable predictor of focused effort is leading by example. Just as parents model appropriate language for the jabbering toddler, organizational leaders should expect their behavior and the organizational values they espouse will be noticed and replicated by others who want similar success. This double-edged sword is highly precarious when inconsistency exists between leader behavior and individual expectations. Also, remain mindful of the realism and practicality of strategic goals. Asking frontline employees to grow sales by 500% over previous years or to recruit hundreds of new employees in an unrealistic period or without support will constrain effort and frustrate an already disenchanted group.

Perhaps you are not in a leadership position or maybe you are interviewing for a new job or promotion. If so, you should test for compatibility between strategy and action by asking direct interview questions. Inquiries about the success of prior strategic plans, information about why people leave the company, and insight regarding management changes provide significant clues about the consistency between talk and action. Some possible interview questions include:

- "Can you provide an example of how leadership follows through on promises?"

- "What employee-centered programs has the company implemented and failed?"

- "What is the top reason for employee turnover?"

The responses to these questions should produce relevant information to help you assess the organization's ability to successfully implement strategy. If the interviewer looks shocked, surprised, balks, or fails to adequately answer your questions, you've likely discovered a good reason to work elsewhere.

***

Leadership Mistake #3

Assuming followers know expectations

For over 20 years, I was accountable for the successful performance of others. In my role as a Human Resources Consultant for some of the world's largest and most successful companies, I was often the person communicating bad news, like telling employees they were on probation or even worse, fired. The infractions ranged from toilet paper theft to the inability to perform basic job duties. Invariably, if the problem was performance-related, most employees expressed surprise and shock upon receiving the feedback. While employee reactions to discipline were possibly contrived to cushion the emotional blow, it was painfully obvious some people were genuinely clueless about company expectations. Many individuals claimed they did not understand how their success was measured, or how their job was linked to the overall company mission. The meetings rarely ended without anger, disgust, or frustration. Supervisors usually claimed employees were negligent, but I knew part of the reason for misalignment was lack of clarity in job expectations.

The mystery of performance requirements is not limited to corporations. The foundation of the university system is based on the elusive notion of "tenure." For those who are unfamiliar with the term or process, tenure is an earned employment category for academic faculty. Depending upon university expectations, over time individuals develop a portfolio of accomplishment that includes teaching, scientific research, and service contributions to the university and community. Each criterion is formally evaluated during the 6th or 7th year of employment. Given the expectations are met, tenure is earned.

For all intents and purposes, tenure guarantees lifetime employment and the designation means faculty are virtually untouchable, provided they don't sell illicit drugs to students or wind up accused of intimacy with farm animals (in the classroom). A frequent complaint from faculty seeking tenure is the lack of documented information concerning the actual requirements to earn this prestigious category of employment. Individuals work for many years shrouded in mystery, uncertain whether their performance will be sufficient to warrant approval after judgment by at least four levels of university bureaucrats who subjectively assess the candidate's tenure portfolio. However, there is one other factor I failed to mention: if you are in a tenure-earning position and don't pass muster at the end of the evaluation period, the university fires you! Therefore, earning tenure is the be-all and end-all for most academic faculty yet written expectations and performance rubrics are typically not provided.

- Unspecified goals
- One-way communication
- No way to exceed targets

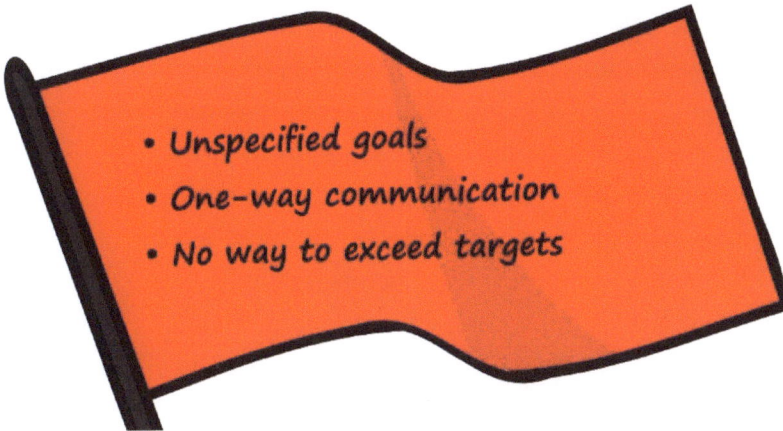

Sadly, the situations described here are not isolated instances of poor leadership, but are more often routine occurrences. Is it possible to have high levels of employee engagement when expectations are vague? The logical answer is "no," but the predictable rebuttal from organizations lacking performance systems is employees should not need to be told what to do. Naysayers contend if someone must be told expectations then they probably aren't qualified for the job. Alternatively, lack of knowledge about job expectations can be attributed to absentee supervision, employee misinterpretations, or lack of communication. Regardless of the underlying reasons for worker uncertainty, the problem is seemingly eliminated through implementation of a "SMART" goal system. The SMART goal system advocates creation of *Specific*, *Measurable*, *Attainable*, *Relevant*, and *Timely* objectives for every role within an organization. The goal criteria are developed and agreed upon by the leader and the individual contributor, *theoretically* eliminating ambiguity and honing employee focus.

Motivational Murder

The key word in the previous paragraph is *"theoretically."* Many organizations routinely use job analysis and job descriptions to communicate position expectations. These systems are relatively effective in outlining what the person will do on a day-to-day basis, with emphasis placed on position outcomes. However, most job analysis and description programs only focus on job-related skills. Critical factors leading to organizational success such as cultural compatibility and motivational beliefs are rarely, if ever, mentioned. This omission of values is surprising considering most instances of organizational mismatch are not based on skill deficits, but rather due to a *"lack of fit"* between the individual and the organization. In practice, lack of fit means a misalignment between individual motives and company beliefs and values. Therefore, the first step toward outlining employee expectations is incorporating motivational factors into the performance management process. Some examples of motivational beliefs that influence performance can be viewed on the *Hack Your Motivation* YouTube channel.

The second reason communicating expectations can go awry is not based upon the job specifics but on *how* the information is communicated. In some organizations, performance plans and objectives do not involve information exchange, but are conducted through top-down edicts from management. There is no discussion or negotiation between supervisor and employee—negating the entire purpose of setting goals and expectations, which is to inspire and motivate exemplary performance while gaining individual commitment to achieve organizational priorities. In some cases, organizations provide no goals or objectives whatsoever. Instead, at the end of the annual performance evaluation period, managers ask employees to conduct a self-evaluation of notable achievements. In these self-evaluation systems, supervisors rate the information drafted by the employee and arbitrarily select some material for inclusion in the employee's performance and development plan. The streamlined procedure often backfires as the employee becomes disenfranchised, not knowing exactly what was expected, why the specific achievements were featured in the evaluation, or why other accomplishments were excluded. Employee uncertainty leads to potential alienation because leaders failed to provide basic and direct communication about how performance is evaluated.

Third, even under the best of conditions, leaders often fail to mention how performance can *exceed* expectations. For those involved in companies, relationships, or any type of partnership where one person or entity evaluates the effectiveness of another, many strive to be more than merely acceptable or sufficient. While some individuals are personally satisfied meeting others' expectations, some of us stake personal reputations on achieving levels of superiority beyond basic standards. Thus, to satisfy the excellence motives of extraordinary performers, it is the leader's obligation to clearly describe achievement levels that exceed standards and how to surpass acceptable performance.

So, what should you do if you don't know the standards necessary to be successful on the job? First, craft job expectations from your point of view. Ask your supervisor to do the same. Exchange notes. If your supervisor balks, reply indicating you will focus on what you wrote absent their response. Be sure to include deadlines for timely completion. If there is agreement to discuss the written expectations, ask the simple question: "How can I *exceed* my job expectations?" Most managers will be hard pressed to provide a specific answer with measurable criteria. Be prepared with objective metrics that accurately reflect your contribution to the organization. If all else fails, solicit support from co-workers who are probably experiencing similar frustrations. Group efforts don't mean ganging up on the boss, rather they are an attempt to brainstorm solutions to a complex issue. Ultimately, it is the responsibility of both parties to know and discuss performance excellence, regardless of the type of role or relationship. If expectations cannot be articulated, the leader has failed.

***

Leadership Mistake #4

Most people are motivated by similar rewards

In the best-selling book "Drive," author Daniel Pink attempts to simplify motivation science by suggesting the superiority of intrinsic over extrinsic motives to instill optimal work performance. When motivated intrinsically, individuals set goals and engage in behavior for reasons related to personal improvement such as satisfying intellectual curiosity, increasing self-esteem, and feeling gratified by accomplishment. Alternatively, behavior is motivated by external forces, including extrinsic rewards such as pay for performance, incentives, and lofty test scores. At deeper levels, materialistic gains can be linked to recognition from others, improved social status, and the ability to secure a reservation in a sold-out hotel. However, unlike Pink, after you read *Hack Your Motivation* you will know when motives are accurately interpreted, ***one size does not fit all***. Simplistic and unitary explanations of motivation are wrong because of the changing nature of motives within people during a task and broad variability between people on different tasks.

Multi-disciplinary research suggests satisfaction of intrinsic needs is more likely to generate and sustain creativity, interest, and enthusiasm toward task completion. In practice, assuming a person will be more or less motivated by a specific incentive type at any given time is as unreliable as predicting the stock market. In other words, leaders who believe certain incentives will be perceived as valuable, coveted, and motivating for an individual will often be wrong. Digesting this concept can be achieved by examining the process of gift-giving. I am highly confident at one time or another while opening a gift you have thought: "Huh? WTF am I going to do with this?" Such a scenario reinforces the range of differences and preferences when it comes to the evaluation of rewards. The horse head squirrel feeder Aunt Sally thought was the perfect gift for you may turn out to be a great white elephant gift at the next company holiday party or used for what I like to call "curb charity."

Instead of generalizing and assuming you know which type of incentive will stimulate performance, when contemplating how to motivate others the savvy leader will consider at least three factors. First, the competency beliefs of the person should be examined. As we know from the *Investment Hack*, people will value certain outcomes over others and performance on some tasks will become part of a person's identity, while results on non-valued objectives are motivationally meaningless with no connection to self-appraisals. If I fail at mopping floors (a non-valued objective), I really don't care. However, if a reader despises my books and posts a YouTube video setting one of my creations on fire (a valued objective), I will severely doubt my writing prowess and feel bad. You can increase your odds that a reward will be valued by providing choice - but be careful. Simply asking individuals to describe what they prefer may at face value appear to be an accurate method of determining preferences. However, keep in mind individuals will often publicly exhibit behaviors and respond in politically-correct ways, while privately embrace different beliefs or undisclosed choices.

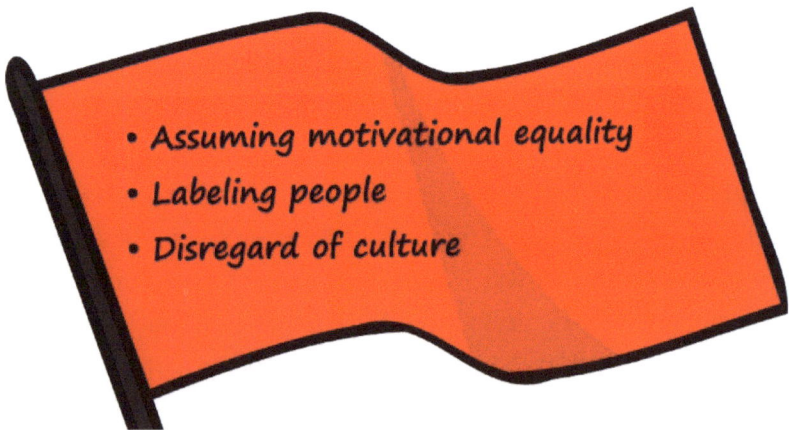

- Assuming motivational equality
- Labeling people
- Disregard of culture

Culture is a second and decisive clue in detecting prevailing influence of rewards on performance. Culture means the typical or normal behaviors, values, and beliefs embraced by a group of individuals. Culture represents much more than ethnic or religious similarities and comprises the values and preferences held by any type of group, ranging from a family or cluster of friends to the ideas and routines considered appropriate within large multi-national corporations or political groups. The advantage of assessing culture is learning the written and implied principles of behavior that govern how people act and what is valued by the group. Thus, we should strive toward aligning rewards with valued cultural behaviors.

As a ludicrous example: if we are determining an appropriate incentive for a group of ministers, we would likely exclude complimentary tickets to a gentleman's club as an appropriate reward. If you think this example is absurd you may be interested to learn many universities are rewarded with government funding based on *graduating more students*, a move that is directly antithetical to the culture and purpose of institutions of higher education: building competency and graduating *qualified individuals equipped for the workforce*. Similarly, many organizations punish employees for not being at their desks at a certain time while paying little attention to the employee's actual productivity, skills, or contribution. Each of these examples demonstrates an incompatibility between desired outcomes and incentives to perform.

A third factor of special relevance to organizations is how individuals are compensated. Conventional wisdom assumes individuals are only marginally motivated by salary, but again, broad generalizations are often incorrect and the impact of monetary rewards should be examined on an individual basis. Salary may be exceptionally motivating when perceptions of unfairness or inequity exist, and removing an injustice is often evaluated as satisfying and inspirational. If you honestly examine your own patterns of behavior, you may admit that you have overstayed a job because of materialistic reasons---it happens. Any consideration of compensation should also examine how individuals contribute to group efforts. Team-based compensation is an effective formula to promote individual and group productivity. While the contingencies of team-based incentives are too lengthy and complicated to discuss here, the most effective systems MUST include both individual and team incentives to promote optimal motivation. Group compensation alone can undermine individual aspects of performance and contribute to the "*free-loader effect*," which happens when group slackers go along for the corporate ride.

***

Leadership Mistake #5

Leaders are not accountable to employees

Google "Boss Rule #1." The search will return one of the most common ideologies in the annals of leadership history and a warped philosophy many leaders, managers, and supervisors embrace without hesitation. Your search likely returned: "*Rule #1 - The Boss is always right, Rule #2 - If the Boss is wrong, see Rule #1*." While this meme may be amusing for some, in practice unilateral decision-making and autocratic leadership reign supreme in many organizations. Leaders who follow this mantra are misguided and operate under pre-historic power motives, which may be appropriate for military generals during combat, but authoritarian leadership style is contrary to success in a matrixed or hierarchical organization.

Leaders who embrace the *"Boss Rule"* are making several judgment errors. First, many individuals in positions of authority mistakenly operate under the presumption that a job title certifies leadership ability. This phenomenon is not surprising considering organizations across industries and disciplines promote people with quality frontline accomplishments into management positions, despite their lack of supervisory or leadership experience. In industry, the best mechanic often becomes a team leader, in sales the person who generates the most revenue typically becomes a manager of junior staff, and in academia the most prolific researcher or best teacher steps up to become an administrator, director, dean or even university president! However, a title and front-line experience certainly does not ensure others will respond favorably to the whims of a newly-appointed leader. Functional knowledge is only one of many skill sets needed to successfully navigate the complex role of motivating performance. Appointed leaders who believe they are qualified to lead based on prior experience in the jobs they are now expected to supervise fail to realize that trust, integrity, and respect are earned qualities that cannot be instilled or designated by the provision of a job title alone.

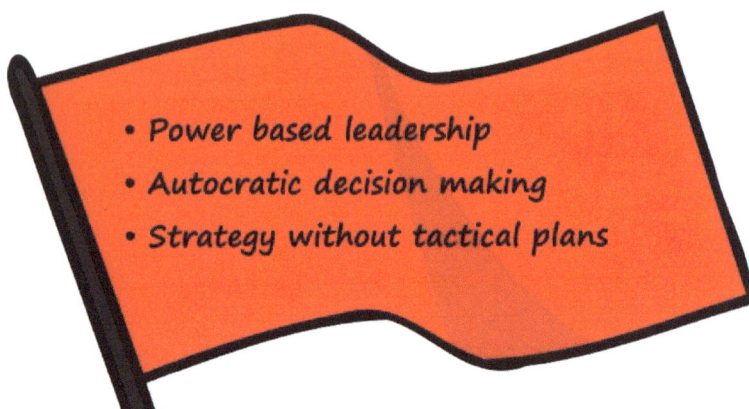

- **Power based leadership**
- **Autocratic decision making**
- **Strategy without tactical plans**

Another common error inexperienced leaders often commit is operating under the forthright premise of being "*employee-centered.*" By most definitions, employee-centered means seeking input of employees before implementing policies or important organizational decisions and empowering employees by giving them "*a voice.*" However, a measurable difference exists between leaders who honestly invite employees to have decision-making input and those who pretend employees are empowered despite pre-determined decisions. For example, imagine an employee committee designed to evaluate prospective job candidates and make recommendations to a hiring official. In this example, committee members would likely feel empowered and motivated to make the best decision if their efforts determined who ultimately earned the job offer. However, how would the committee members feel if the hiring official suggested in writing a certain candidate would be perfect for the job, *before* the committee even interviewed the candidate? Readers of *Hack Your Motivation* know from the *Selling Hack* that committee members would feel useless with little motivation to invest effort in candidate evaluation because the hiring official had clearly already made the decision for the team. Committee members couldn't possibly make an unbiased decision based upon the leader's pre-interview endorsement. The presumption of empowerment and the appearance of listening to frontline employees would backfire, creating animosity, hostility, and lack of trust.

A third lethal error committed by inexperienced leaders is communicating strategic goals and long-term vision without considering implementation issues. While leaders should clearly articulate organizational strategy and give employees an opportunity to determine how goals will be reached, there should be consideration of how plans will be initiated. Discussion should include which short-term and attainable objectives must be met to achieve the strategic vision. From a motivational perspective, strategic goals without concrete operational plans give employees the impression of being set up for failure. Long-term objectives lacking practicality completely disregard the *Milestone Hack*, which states realistic and attainable interim goals enhance performance and are essential for long-term growth. For example, if a leader wants a 50% revenue increase within three years, there should also be discussion of marketing and advertising resources, additions to staff, and interim plans to support the leader's vision. Without details, frontline workers may feel overwhelmed and skeptical leading to disengagement and potential employee turnover.

The leadership liabilities described above revolve around the same misguided principle where a leader believes their role is to dictate objectives with the expectation others will obediently follow through and figure out how to get the job done. Unsuccessful leaders may fail to realize that even when employees *appear* committed to company objectives, ancillary leadership support is necessary to maintain motivation. Providing support means securing plentiful material resources, but also assumes an investment in personal development to generate positive morale through leadership action. Instead of perpetually demanding results, forthright leaders should instead ask "How can my efforts contribute to the success of those I lead?" or "What can I do to make strategic implementation easier?" Assessing leader support can be accomplished during the interviewing process. Ask questions like "How do you motivate your staff?" or "What was the termination reasoning the last time you fired someone?" Answers to these types of questions reveal what your future boss values and what you can expect as a prospective employee. Ultimately, the leader is accountable to everyone in the organization. Effective leaders understand the success of an organization is attributable to the team, but organizational failure is the onus of the leader.

***

Leadership Mistake #6

Pressure motivates superior performance

While goofing off in my office one day, a colleague stopped by and took a seat. My co-worker proceeded to share a story about a meeting she attended where our boss raised her voice at one of the attendees. Curious, I inquired about what prompted the boss's rude and unprofessional behavior. My colleague explained the boss was dismayed over an employee's lack of preparation and wanted everyone in the meeting to know she did not approve. I was rather disturbed a public berating occurred, but then I remembered other similar instances and subtle overtures people in authority use that could be perceived as intimidating. I visualized annoyed facial expressions and signs of impatience suggested by body language. I knew from a supervisory seminar that looking at your watch or glancing back at a computer screen while having a conversation were clear signs of boredom or dismissal.

The boss's behavior intrigued me so much I conducted some research. I uncovered a wealth of literature about covert, yet meaningful transgressions that occur when people in power exert pressure on others. Some of these negative comments and actions can have racial or ethnic overtones and are commonly referred to as micro-aggressions because they subtly intimidate the recipient. However, non-racially motivated comments and veiled messages occur regularly in workplaces as seemingly well-intentioned supervisors make incidental comments designed and intended to motivate, but are perceived as hostile, intimidating, and stressful.

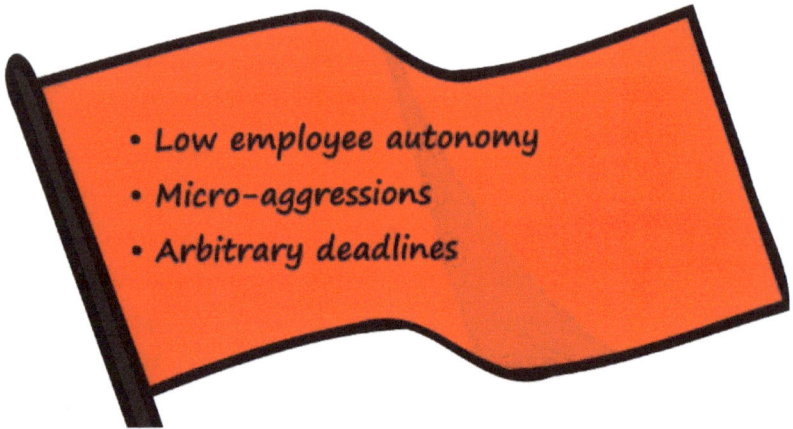

- Low employee autonomy
- Micro-aggressions
- Arbitrary deadlines

How we react to these pressured overtures is discretionary. The *Water to Wine Hack* in *Hack Your Motivation* reveals reactions to stress are subjective. Fortunately, some of us have enough practice and knowledge of emotional control strategies and are well equipped to deal with day-to-day stress in the form of oblivious bosses who underestimate the impact of their words and actions. Others with less work experience or more antagonistic working conditions may see performance quickly deteriorate under the slightest perception of supervisory pressure. Regardless, everyone has a breaking point. When that point is reached, performance suffers because cognitive resources are dedicated toward dealing with the anxiety and perception of pressure to meet the boss's demands, instead of focusing on the task at hand. In *Hack Your Motivation*, I described an episode when my boss, Mr. Trellis, lashed out at me and flung all his papers on the floor during a meltdown. Sadly, many bosses operate under the false presumption that setting irrational deadlines or intimidating employees will stimulate performance, when in reality performing under pressure often decreases motivation and task commitment because the event is perceived as overly stressful. The pressure cultivates anxiety rather than promoting productivity.

While moderate levels of task-based challenge can arouse awareness and heighten task performance, leaders who use stress, pressure, intimidation, or hierarchical power to motivate constituents will eventually fail. The most successful leaders take decisive and measurable action to insulate employees from the stress and pressure of senior executives and uncontrollable market forces. The first step toward eliminating implied pressure is critically examining the leader's behavior. Like many aspects of emotional management, leadership behaviors can be on autopilot, seemingly operating intuitively. Taking a step back and critically evaluating verbal and written messages can derail perception of pressure before it starts.

Second, leaders should recognize not all employees are cognitively equipped to handle pressure and some will react negatively to challenging working conditions. Third, it is a leader's obligation to provide stress management training. Program content should include how to develop resilience and confidence and also address how to respond to a supervisor or manager who may be unaware how their speech and actions impact employee motivation. Finally, in the event a person has coping issues dealing with the leadership style of a direct supervisor, confidential mechanisms should be in place to anonymously report behavior that may be considered unprofessional and potentially unethical.

***

Leadership Mistake #7

Misalignment among organizational systems

An effective approach to determine the ideal qualities needed to motivate others is accomplished by asking a co-worker the simple question: "Describe the best boss or teacher you have ever had." Responses to the inquiry usually include:

- Fair

- Honest

- Authentic

- Communicates well

- Empathetic

- Kind

- Good business acumen

- Strong technical knowledge

- Enthusiastic

- Motivated

While the answers to the "best boss" question may seem predictable, descriptions exclude the organizational conditions needed to enable leadership excellence. To thrive and reach our potential as individuals and leaders we need a nurturing and caring environment. Absent a supportive culture, personal development may be limited despite exceptional individual motivation to

29

perform. A similar paradigm applies to organizational maturation and success: unless certain systems and procedures are in place, business prosperity and corresponding leadership development will be hampered.

Determining a direct connection between the cause of company success and how the company is managed is a slippery slope because there are so many fluctuating factors that contribute to business growth. However, listing factors contributing to organizational success is relatively straight-forward. Abundant research across disciplines confirms profitable companies have strong financial integrity, engage in ethical decision-making, are strategically positioned within their industry, foster innovation and creativity, have low employee turnover, and demonstrate employee-centered management. Organizational success profiles also include personal or non-financial factors leading to favorable company evaluations. Non-financial factors are more subjective and harder to quantify but include providing employees with job-specific autonomy, offering training opportunities, affording flexible working conditions and schedules, and supporting an appropriate work/life balance consistent with employee expectations. Another often overlooked factor related to earning positive evaluations is congruity among organizational systems. In this case "systems" refers to human resources functions, such policies related to the selection, placement, and promotion of employees, as well as continuity among compensation, benefits, and personal development practices.

Let's take a closer look at how systemic alignment, or lack thereof, may impact employee motivation. Stanley, a recent college grad with an accounting degree is hoping to work with one of the top accounting firms in the world and seeking a position as an auditor. His job will be to advise clients to follow statutory regulations and verify that financial records are suitable to withstand Internal Revenue Service scrutiny. Stanley answered an Internet advertisement and received a telephone interview where he was asked routine questions about availability, interests, salary requirements, teamwork, and his preferred career path. His responses were sufficient to warrant an in-person interview, where three different managers and a prospective co-worker quizzed him on questions like those he encountered during the phone screen. After about an hour, Stanley went home reflecting upon the experience and was excited about the job opportunity because of the firm's reputation and the potential for career growth. The position was also attractive because each person who interviewed Stanley emphasized how the firm valued employee development and strived to retain the best and brightest employees for the long-term. Stanley wanted the job, despite not knowing what he had to accomplish to be successful at the company and to eventually become a firm Partner who could easily earn $500,000 or more per year.

A few weeks later, Stanley received an acceptable job offer. His annual salaried wages would be $52,000 and included two weeks paid vacation per year. On his first day, he went through orientation and read lots of company manuals while awaiting his first client placement. He was assigned to a location far from the home office and would need to leave for work almost an hour earlier than he originally planned. Over the next two months, he regularly worked 12-hour days. His effort was primarily devoted towards reading financial statements for accuracy, along with a group of six other auditors, all of whom had been hired at the same time as Stanley. Over time Stanley became tired, cranky, and suspicious. He began to regret his decision and believed it was the firm's strategy to hire more people than needed, because inevitably some would quit. He began to think his perception of hard work and what the company expected were misaligned. Stanley went to Human Resources (HR) to inquire why he always needed to work 12-hour days. The HR Manager explained the firm makes money by billing out employees to clients at higher rates than employees are paid. The more auditors and hours that could be billed on a job, the bigger the company profit. The HR manager also told Stanley "If you plan to get promoted at this company, expect to work the same schedule for at least the next two years." Two days later, a frustrated and disillusioned Stanley quit.

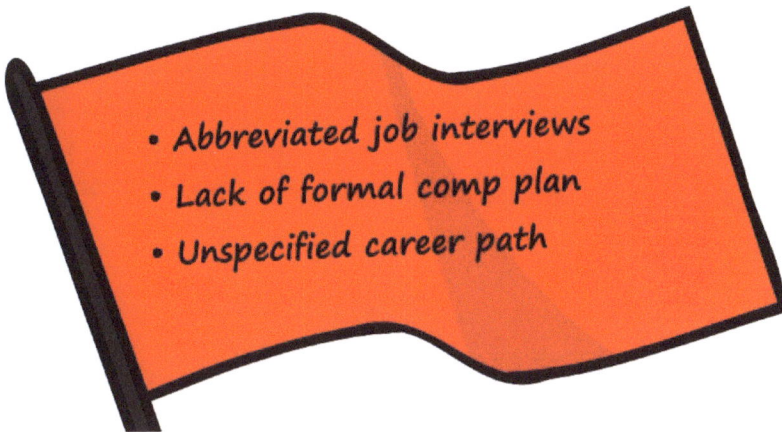

- Abbreviated job interviews
- Lack of formal comp plan
- Unspecified career path

The above story is true and often standard operating procedure for many of the top public accounting firms. While you may not agree with the described business model or strategy, what mattered most from Stanley's motivational perspective was the dissimilarity in values between the organization and his personal belief system. Stanley thought working 12-hour days for extended periods was excessive and not a factor that should be considered for job promotion. The firm believed their business model was ingenious, because it made a profit on each auditor billed out to a client, assuming the company could hire enough graduates to replace the ones who quit prematurely. If Stanley or anyone else wanted to make it to the coveted Partner level, they would have to put in their time and pay their dues.

There was a disconnect between Stanley and the firm based on working expectations and which behaviors were required for personal success and job progression. Stanley felt used by the company. The company probably believed Stanley wasn't cut out to be successful in a public accounting firm. Maybe Stanley didn't ask the right questions during his interview, or maybe the company employees withheld information because they feared Stanley would be frightened away and they needed to hire someone fast. Ultimately, it's irrelevant because Stanley's brief tenure occurred due to incompatibility with the organizational culture and lack of congruity among compensation, benefit, career development systems, and day-to-day working conditions.

From an organizational perspective, Stanley's motivation to endure routine working conditions suffered because the recruiting and evaluation process was a mismatch with Stanley's view of employee development. Perhaps the recruiter should have discussed the business model in-depth or asked different questions of Stanley such as "What will you sacrifice to reach your career aspirations?" Ideally, the compensation plan at the company should have been geared towards incentivizing employees to work more hours, such as providing a retention bonus or a special time off plan when certain billable hour thresholds were exceeded.

Other solutions may have prevented Stanley's departure including more forthright disclosure from interviewers about how to be successful within the company culture. Alternatively, the company staked their business livelihood on hiring volume, not hiring the *right type* of candidate who wanted to endure excessive work hours to reap the long-term financial gain associated with promotion. Deciding who to blame for Stanley's departure is pragmatically useless, however, knowing in advance which interview questions to ask reaps enormous benefits for the employee and the employer before an employment decision is finally made.

***

The purpose of outlining the seven motivational killers was two-fold. First, as an aspiring superstar, you want to avoid making the motivational errors that often lead to the downfall of your rivals. Second, even if you are unsure of your direction, unemployed, or not a boss, partner, parent, or anyone else who is responsible for others, someday you may need to avoid these mistakes to demonstrate your leadership ability. Regardless, pay heed to these potential errors when you evaluate employment offers. Whether you are seeking a leadership role or not, you should actively test to determine whether your prospective employer is making the dreadful mistakes described here. When in doubt, keep looking, or you may become a victim of a naïve or ill-informed leader who rebukes some of the most ubiquitous findings in the history of motivational and organizational science.

Now, you have an important decision to make. There are over 50 other strategies NOT described in this book that you can use to enhance your personal and professional effectiveness. *Hack Your Motivation* is the only book completely based on science that gives you the competitive advantage to attain your goals quicker and with far less effort than your uninformed peers. Written in an entertaining and informative style, and guaranteed to make you laugh while you learn, the book also includes 30 video segments that provide instant learning for those on the go. Get your copy *now*!

***

Follow me on Twitter @ifoundmo for daily updates on leadership, performance, motivation, and learning.

***

Also, up your performance by reading my Psychology Today blog.

***

For more information about Dr. Hoffman review the University of Central Florida website, Google Scholar, or his Amazon.com author page. Feel free to email hackyourmotivation@gmail.com with any comments or questions.

Until next time, *GO HACK YOURSELF!*

Notes

www.ingramcontent.com/pod-product-compliance
Lightning Source LLC
Chambersburg PA
CBHW041223270326
41933CB00001B/17